THE UNOFFICIAL *FORTNITE*®
SURVIVAL GUIDE

BUILDING STRUCTURES AND COLLECTING RESOURCES IN *FORTNITE*®

JANET HARVEY

Enslow Publishing
101 W. 23rd Street
Suite 240
New York, NY 10011
USA

enslow.com

Published in 2020 by Enslow Publishing, LLC
101 W. 23rd Street, Suite 240, New York, NY 10011

Library of Congress Cataloging-in-Publication Data

Names: Hamilton, Tracy Brown.
Title: Building structures and collecting resources in Fortnite® / Tracy Brown Hamilton
Description: New York : Enslow Publishing, 2020. | Series: The unofficial
Fortnite® survival guide | Includes glossary and index.
Identifiers: ISBN 9781978517073 (pbk.) | ISBN 9781978517097
(library bound) | ISBN 9781978517080 (6 pack)
Subjects: LCSH: Fortnite Battle Royale (Game)—Juvenile literature. | Imaginary
wars and battles—Juvenile literature. | Video games—Juvenile literature.
Classification: LCC GV1469.35.F67 H36 2020 | DDC 794.8—dc23

Fortnite is a trademark of Epic Games, and its use in this book does not
imply a recommendation or endorsement of this title by Epic Games.

Printed in the United States of America

To Our Readers: We have done our best to make sure all website addresses in this book
were active and appropriate when we went to press. However, the author and the publisher
have no control over and assume no liability for the material available on those websites
or on any websites they may link to. Any comments or suggestions can be sent by email to
customerservice@enslow.com.

CONTENTS

INTRODUCTION

If you're reading this strategy guide, chances are you are already one of the two hundred million gamers worldwide who are obsessed with *Fortnite*. Since its release in 2017, *Fortnite*

has become one of the most popular games on the planet, mainly due to the success of its multiplayer strategy game, *Fortnite: Battle Royale.*

The original *Fortnite* started out as a four-player cooperative survival shooter game, in which players had to build shelters and defend themselves from marauding zombies on a post-apocalyptic Earth.

Both games focus a lot on building structures. Players who use building as part of their winning strategy tend to last longer and win battles. With this guide, you can grow your building skills beyond the basics and learn how to use building as a tool to get that coveted Victory Royale.

Visitors at E3 (Electronic Entertainment Expo) in Los Angeles check out the latest *Fortnite* news at the Epic Games booth.

CHAPTER 1

The Nuts and Bolts of Building in *Fortnite*

To build, go into the Build menu and take a look at the controls. (Depending on which platform you are playing on, your controls will be slightly different.) To build structures, you'll be choosing to create with four basic "types" of components: floors, walls, roofs, and stairs. In the Build menu, you will see shapes that represent those components in four slots. The fifth slot will be filled with special items you collect as loot, called Traps.

Using those controls will lay down a basic floor, wall, roof, or stairs. But once you have the basics, you can edit the wall or floor by selecting the element, which reveals a tile grid that you can modify. By adding and removing tiles, you can edit the original structure, add doors and windows, or create a set of stairs.

Depending on what device you use to play *Fortnite*, your building tools menu might look slightly different.

Practice in the Playground

It takes practice to create different structure types quickly, so you'll want to hone your building skills before you try to create elaborate structures in the middle of combat. The best way to do that is to switch to Playground mode. Playground mode is what game developers call a sandbox mode. It allows players to explore the map and experiment with building structures. Playground mode allows you to do that in *Fortnite:* Battle Royale without having to worry about people attacking you!

SAFETY

When interacting with people online, you should practice the same principles of safety that you would in the real world. If you don't know someone in real life, you shouldn't add that person as a friend in the game or on your gaming platform. Don't give anyone you don't know your name or address. And if someone you don't know becomes abusive or bullies you, you can exit the game and talk to an adult or report that person to Epic Games, the company that makes *Fortnite*. There's a Report Player option in the game.

If you experience bullying in *Fortnite*, there is help available. Contact Epic Games through the Report function, and tell an adult.

The *Fortnite* Creative mode allows players to build to their hearts' content and even create mini-games.

Currently, Playground is a limited time mode (LTM), which means it appears only once a month or so. So if you don't see it right now, don't worry—it'll be back soon!

CHAPTER 2

Wood, Metal, and Stone, Oh My!

To create any kind of structure in *Fortnite*, you'll need three building materials: wood, stone, and metal. These three materials can be used to build any structure. They have different properties when it comes to building, but one thing is for sure: You need a lot of all of them all the time.

One thing to be aware of is that materials have "health" in the game, just like you do. The health of materials refers to its durability against attack. Different materials make for quicker or slower builds as well. You can build faster with wood than

Gather materials whenever you can. When trouble calls you'll want to be ready to build!

you can with metal, for example—but metal makes for a more solid, durable structure.

Wood

Wood is the lightest and easiest to get of the materials in *Fortnite*. It has a five-second build time per panel, a starting health of 100, and a max health of 200. It's a good basic thing to build with when you just want to put a structure together quickly.

You can easily scavenge wood by chopping up trees and other wooden things like logs, or you can even take it from previously built wooden structures.

Stone

Stone is the mid-level building material in *Fortnite*. It has a twelve-second build time per panel, a starting health of 90, and a max health of 300.

The best way to get stone is to mine it from boulders with your Pickaxe. You can also destroy brick walls to scavenge stone. Or you can just wait for someone else to destroy a brick wall, then kill that person and take the dropped loot!

BEST SCAVENGING PRACTICES

Scavenging is one of your primary goals in *Fortnite*, and if you want to make it anywhere in the game, you'll need to keep your backpack, also known as your inventory, well supplied with construction materials. That means you're always on the lookout to harvest wood, stone, and metal from objects you encounter in the game.

Just remember that people can see and hear you when you are swinging your Pickaxe at that brick wall or metal pipe. If you are scavenging metal from a car, you might set off a car alarm, which will draw enemies to your location! So just be careful, and be aware of your surroundings.

Your backpack has slots for weapons, gear, healing meds, grenades, ammo, and building materials.

Metal

Metal is the most durable material in *Fortnite*, but with a twenty-second build time per panel, you might want to use it sparingly, especially in the early stages of the game. It has a starting health of 80 but an ending health of 400.

Cities are the most abundant source of metal, where you can scavenge from metal objects such as pipes, metal poles, or cars and other

Cities are great places to scavenge for metal, but be careful about making too much noise!

vehicles. But out in the forest, you can also find stashes of metal ore in caves and mine for resources there.

Each material has advantages and disadvantages, depending on your situation. For example, wooden structures are fastest to construct but more likely to collapse under enemy fire. Stone and metal are also good for the base of any high towers you want to construct since enemies can still topple your structures by attacking the bottom. (Oh yeah, and if you are on the tower when it gets knocked down? You *will* die.)

Speaking of towers, let's look at some of the cool things you can build with these simple elements!

CHAPTER 3

Basic Structures and Why You Want to Build Them

One of the best things you can do in *Fortnite: Battle Royale* is to get in the habit of building a quick cube as soon as you start taking shots. You can then edit the wall from inside, creating doors, windows, or even an elaborate trap for an opponent.

The Panic Wall

Here is a basic defensive move: Someone throws up a quick wall during a combat encounter to buy himself or herself a few extra seconds in the game. It's a simple, quick strategy. Just construct a standard wall between you and whoever is attacking you.

The first step to surviving in *Fortnite*: Learn to build a panic wall!

The Panic Ramp

Only slightly more complex than the Panic Wall, this structure is a great way to get the upper hand on an opponent quickly by getting up higher and implementing a surprise attack.

Construct a panic ramp by setting up at least three standard walls, then place a set of stairs between them. The slope of the ramp allows

17

If you need to get good altitude, a sniper tower lets you get high up, fast.

you to dip in and out of enemy sights and attack from above in a defended position.

A V-Shaped Ramp

Similar to Panic Ramps, a V-Shaped Ramp is basically two Panic Ramps that meet in the middle. If you box yourself in and create two ramps across from each other, you are in a fully defended position.

Sniper Tower

What's better than a fully defended V-Shape Ramp? Why, a V-Shape Ramp that's way up high in the air, of course!

To construct a Sniper Tower, box yourself in with four standard walls. Build a set of stairs, move up higher, and then build another box and another stair level. Do this until you have a good height or you run out of building materials. Then just wait up there in comfort, picking off other players as they move toward you.

CHAPTER 4

Healing Rooms and Other Strategic Building Uses

Building is useful in combat, but it comes in handy in other situations, too. As you get around the island and collect loot and resources or try to get away from monsters, here are some other ways building skills can save you.

Reaching Higher Ground: Stairways, Platforms, and Panic Floors

Sometimes, there's a mountain between you and the place you want to get to. Or a big building. That's when a series of stairs and platforms can get you from point A to point B. As long as nobody is shooting at you, you can

Stairways aren't just a means to get from one place to another. They can be a good survival strategy.

build a pretty elaborate structure just to get up a mountainside!

Similarly, if you are falling off a mountain, a quick-thinking build of a floor can actually save you from falling to your death.

IT'S A TRAP! OR HOW TO BUNGEE JUMP TO THE OTHER SIDE OF THE ISLAND

Traps were a big part of the original *Fortnite* game, used primarily as a way of defending your team's fort from monsters. Once they migrated to *Fortnite: Battle Royale* and got used in combat, players found new ways to use Traps that cranked the fun up to 1,000!

For instance, instead of using a Bouncer Trap or a Launch Pad as a way to eject an enemy from your location, you can also use it to launch *yourself* to another location. A combination of Launch Pads and glider deployment can take you far from the reach of even the most persistent opponent!

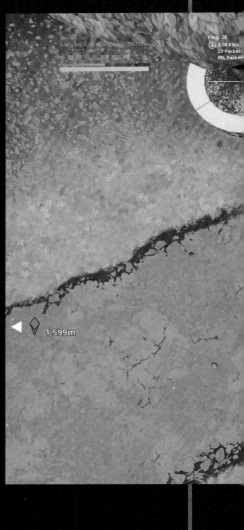

Grenades, Grapplers, and Launch Pads offer unique ways to travel across the Battle Royale map as fast as possible.

Healing Rooms: The Gift of Fire

One type of structure you can start using immediately in your *Fortnite:* Battle Royale gameplay, regardless of your ability, is Healing Rooms. When you've taken a lot of damage, Healing Rooms give you a place to hide while you heal.

To build one, you'll need a Cozy Campfire. The Cozy Campfire is a rare, one-use Trap that

The Cozy Campfire is a great one-use healing item that can heal your whole party. But be careful: the glow is visible through walls!

heals any surrounding players at a rate of 2 Hit Points, or HP, per second. This can come in very handy, particularly in later stages of the game, when damage is the worst and you and your teammates may be running out of health recovery items.

To build a Healing Room, put up four walls and a roof around you, your teammates, and the campfire. That's it. Try to find an inconspicuous place to put your Healing Room because you only get one use out of the Cozy Campfire.

Stairway to Heaven— the Sky's the Limit

There's great strategic value to just getting higher up than your opponent. Being above the fray gives you an edge, and you may sometimes see two towers next to each other going higher and higher into the sky as two players try to edge each other out for the high ground.

How high can you go? Well, there's one strategy that basically involves going up and up until you can't go any farther. The Stairway to Heaven may be unreliable as a strategy, and many have tried and failed. But if you master it, you can actually win a Victory Royale without firing a single shot!

First, you'll need to gather as much wood as you possibly can the minute you land in the game. Try to land in a place where wood is plentiful because being able to get it fast and easy is the name of the game with this strategy. Max out your inventory of wood as fast as you can—999 wood is as much as you can carry. Then start building a giant staircase.

At some point, you will not be able to build any higher. That's when you start building platforms toward the eye of the storm as fast as you can. If you stay ahead of the storm, you can survive until the end of the game and be the last one standing. That is, unless someone with a rocket launcher decides to ruin your day!

The next time you are in the game and you can't find the other person on the island... look up. Chances are, your opponent has the higher ground.

The building mechanics in *Fortnite* are versatile, and you can build almost anything you can think of—and the sky's the limit!

GLOSSARY

DAMAGE Any change to the state of an object, usually a physical object, that degrades it away from its original state.

HEALING The process of regenerating health, or HP, in a game; players usually heal over time through rest or by consuming certain items, such as healing potions or first aid kits.

HEALTH The name given to an attribute assigned to characters and objects in video games that indicates their ability to remain functional within the game.

HIT POINTS These are units that measure how much damage has been done to a character's health or how many that character has left before he or she is defeated. Abbreviated HP.

INVENTORY A collection of items obtained by the player in the game; in *Fortnite*, the player's inventory is what is in his or her backpack.

LOOT Items that can be obtained by the player, such as in-game currency or gold, weapons, materials, or special equipment.

MAP This is a term that refers to the actual terrain of the game—an area, stage, or zone that is the total space available to the player during the course of completing the objective.

MAX OUT To fill your inventory or points with the maximum number allowed in the game.

MECHANICS Game mechanics refers to available actions, or systems of actions, within a game that a user might apply to achieve an objective.

MENU A menu is a set of options or commands presented to the user in the form of a graphic user interface, which allows the user to access information about the program functions available to the user and execute those functions.

MODE In a game, this refers to different states the player is in in the game, such as Build Mode or Combat Mode.

SANDBOX A game mode in which minimal limitations are placed on the player, the idea being that the player is allowed to roam freely and select tasks at will.

FOR MORE INFORMATION

American Esports
Website: https://americanesports.net

Epic Games
Website: http://www.epicgames.com

Ontario Esports League (OESL)
Website: https://www.oesl.ca

Toronto Esports Club
Website: http://www.torontoesports.gg

Twitch
Website: http://www.twitch.tv

Youth Esports of North America
Website: https://www.youthesportsamerica.com

FOR FURTHER READING

Chriscoe, Sharon. *Choosing Your Costume in* Fortnite. New York, NY: Rosen Publishing, 2019.

Epic Games. FORTNITE *(Official): Battle Royale Survival Guide*. New York, NY: Little Brown Books, 2019.

Gregory, Josh. Fortnite *Beginner's Guide*. Ann Arbor, MI: Cherry Lake Publishing, 2019.

Gregory, Josh. Fortnite *Building*. Ann Arbor, MI: Cherry Lake Publishing, 2019.

Hawkins, Josh. Fortnite *Battle Royale Guide: Tips, Tricks and More!* Roseville, CA: Prima Publishing, 2018.

Kuhn, Damien. *The* Fortnite *Guide to Staying Alive*. Kansas City, MO: Andrews McMeel Publishing, 2018.

Pro Gamer Guide. Fortnite *for Kids: 3 Books in 1: Underground Tips & Secrets to Become a* Fortnite *God & Win Battle Royale LIKE THE PROs*. Pro Gamer Guide, 2018.

INDEX

About the Author

Janet Harvey has worked in the game industry as a writer and narrative game designer, first at Sony Online Entertainment as a quest and dialogue writer for the DC Universe Online MMORPG and later for Zynga and Portalarium. She'd like to thank her nephew, ranked player Coti Harvey, for teaching her how to play *Fortnite:* Battle Royale and for sharing his tips and tricks on how to achieve a Victory Royale!

Photo Credits

Cover PixelShot/Shutterstock.com; pp. 4–5 Christian Petersen/ Getty Images; p. 7 Lukmanazis/Shutterstock.com; pp. 8–9 Rawpixel/iStock/Getty Images Plus/Getty Images.

Design & Layout: Brian Garvey; Editor: Bethany Bryan; Photo Researcher: Nicole DiMella; *Fortnite* Consultant: Sam Keppeler